I0164539

Women Are People!

Women Are People!

Alice Duer Miller

MINT EDITIONS

Women Are People! was first published in 1917.

This edition published by Mint Editions 2021.

ISBN 9781513283593 | E-ISBN 9781513288611

Published by Mint Editions®

**MINT
EDITIONS**

minteditionbooks.com

Publishing Director: Jennifer Newens
Design & Production: Rachel Lopez Metzger
Project Manager: Micaela Clark
Typesetting: Westchester Publishing Services

Contents

TREACHEROUS TEXTS

"The basis of our political systems is the right of the people to make and to alter their constitutions of government."

—GEORGE WASHINGTON: *Farewell Address*

"The people's government, made for the people, made by the people, and answerable to the people."

—DANIEL WEBSTER: *Second Speech on Foot's Amendment*

"When we say: 'We, the people, do ordain and establish, etc.,' it is not an unmeaning flourish. The expression declares in a practical manner the principles of this Constitution. It is ordained and established by the people themselves."

—JUDGE WILSON, *in the Pennsylvania convention to consider the Constitution of the United States*

"American women will win the vote, because their campaign has been polite, dignified and tactful."

When the Barons faced King John
    They were civil as could be,
Doffed the crowns they all had on,—
    They were well, they said, and he?
Thus their liberty was won,
    Pretty manners set them free.

When the Commons killed the King,
    Their behaviour was the same.
"Yes," they said, to draw the sting,
    "Really, sire, it's a shame!"
For they knew the slightest thing
    Rough or rude would lose the game.

Washington was most polite
    To the British long ago,
Said he fancied he was right,
    But of course one couldn't know.
Had he tried to sulk or fight,
    They'd have thought him simply low.

These examples, ladies all,
    Should control your every act.
Never argue, nor recall
    Any crude, unwelcome fact.
Revolutions rise and fall
    By the rebels' social tact.

The Selfish Creatures

"In this age of discontent, hundreds of thousands of girls, who have no necessity to support themselves, leave home in order to win pin money."

—Anti-suffrage leaflet. Apply to G. D. M., Albany

I stopped to ask a scrub-woman:
    "Why labour like a man?
You cannot feed your children? Well,
    There must be some one can."
She said: "I merely work because
    I need a feather fan."

I went to a steam laundry,
    And asked with smile polite:
"Ladies, why will you work so late?"
    They said: "We think it right
To buy our opera cloaks ourselves,
    And so we work at night."

Observe how nagging women are:
    Their work is just a feint
To make Man feel inadequate,
    And selfish—which he ain't.
True womanhood would rather starve,
    And starve without complaint!

To Chivalry

"I wonder if fanatical feminists, male and female, ever stop to ask themselves what will happen when the romance of sex is forgotten, or lost sight of, in the furious struggle between men and women which universal suffrage is sure to bring."

—The Phœnix

Chivalry, I don't abuse you,
    Not at all—the only rub
Is that those who praise you, use you
    Very often as a club.

As a club or stick of candy,
    As a punishment or prize,
Finding you extremely handy
    When they want to sermonise.

Chivalry, they say you'll linger
    Only where the girls obey;
Where they show the smallest ginger
    Instantly you fly away.

Many a stern, relentless Anti
    Threatens us poor suffragettes
As a mother tells how Santy
    Naughty children quite forgets.

Yet in spite of all their talking,
    In a day dream, in a trance,
Every day I see you walking
    Arm in arm with old romance.

Every Age

"Oh," cried the old men,
  "The times are full of danger,
And chivalry is dying,
  Its funeral knell has rung;
Love to these young men
  Is utterly a stranger,
Love, that was so fine a thing
  When you and I were young."

"Yes," said the women,
  "The girls have now no mystery,
No modesty to beckon,
  No graces to be sung;
This will be called
  The darkest age in history,
That killed love, the true love
  We loved when we were young."

The young men and maidens,
  With pity in their glances,
They looked upon their elders,
  And, oh, their hearts were wrung!
"How sweet, but how unreal
  Were all their old romances,
For true love is our love,
  While you and I are young!"

The Demise of Chivalry

*"Would it not be a little more just to state that for her taxes this woman
receives police protection, fire protection. . . pure food inspection, and
ash and garbage removed?"*

—Letter of president of the Hudson River
Association Opposed to Woman Suffrage

The courteous policeman on my beat
Who always helps me cross the crowded street,
    Had I the ballot—as I understand—
Would throw me underneath the horses' feet.

The garbage man, whose wise, efficient plan
Is daily to remove my garbage can,
    Would pass me by, all coldness and neglect,
If he should catch me voting like a man.

But one there is who will not change, I know,
However far astray we women go,
    Who questions not of woman's sphere or charm—
The tax collector never answers no.

The Code

"We women are not supposed to be humorous, I know."

—Anti-suffrage speech

Ladies, true to the tradition
    Of the ivy and the oak,
Never make the dark admission
    That you see a joke!

Laugh and smile, for that's beguiling,
    If the teeth are good;
But not knowing why you're smiling—
    That's true womanhood.

Humour must remain a stranger
    To the loving female mind,
If we would avoid all danger
    Of a thought unkind.

Chivalry would go to Hades
    Very, very quickly then.
Men may laugh at us poor ladies;
    We must not at men.

Liberty

A distinguished opponent has been converted to the principles of woman suffrage. Under the title "Personal Liberty" he writes in Case and Comment: *"American freedom is the child of American democracy. It involves equal rights and equal duties. . . The state on the one hand should refrain scrupulously from giving to any individual or association advantages which are denied to others. All should be on an equal plane of opportunity as far as the law can give it."*

O Liberty, how many men there are
    Who do you honour in a flowing phrase,
    In martial measures and in patriot lays,
Invoking you as goddess and as star;
Though fire and cruelty and bloodshed mar
    Your pathways, every deed of yours they praise
    So they were done in long forgotten days,
Or rumoured in strange lands, unknown and far;
But when you first approach them, when you turn
    On their pale eyes your eyes' unwavering light,
        When they perceive you—enemy to peace
And easy comfort, dangerous and stern,
    They fly before you, crying in their fright:
        "Arrest this wild-eyed jade! Police! Police!"

On the Recent Good News from Kansas

"The State of Kansas is out of debt."

—Press clipping

Kansas is out of debt!
Oh, when the anti-speaker, stern and tense,
Declares that woman has no business sense,
Describes the wild taxation we shall pay,
When woman, flighty woman, has her way,
Paints the financial smashes,
The failures and crashes
That must ensue when woman takes a hand
In governing the land;
Don't be annoyed; just smile and say:
   "But yet
      Kansas is out of debt."

Kansas is out of debt,—
Kansas where women vote; whereas to date
New York, the proud, the rich, the Empire State,
With its magnificently male finance,
And business interests that have looked askance
On women taking any part
In matters other than the heart,
New York has not, from recent information,
Met every obligation;
New York, which prudently will only let
The sex of business experts vote. And yet
      New York's not out of debt!

Protect the Shrine

Mr. Webb, of North Carolina, recently voted against a bill to restrict child labour. But he said in his anti-suffrage speech: "The most sacred and potential spot on earth is the fireside shrine, and over this shrine the devoted mother presides, the uncrowned queen."

Oh, home is a shrine for a mother, it may be,
But a shrine is no place for a promising baby.
Small children are fond of disturbance and riot,
But a shrine should be sacred and lonely and quiet.

CHORUS

O, come all ye factory owners, combine;
Though the world misinterpret your noble design,
Keep children away from a spot so divine,
So potential and pure as the fireside shrine.

O woman, O mother, we love and respect you,
As queen and as goddess we long to protect you,
And how can we give you a pleasanter day
Than by keeping your dear little children away?

CHORUS

O, come all ye factory owners, combine;
Protecting the home is your own special line,
Since childhood is boist'rous, we firmly decline
To permit it to trouble the fireside shrine.

BOTHERATION

"Why do you come here and bother us?"

—Chairman Webb, at the suffrage hearing in Washington

Girls, girls, the worst has happened;
    Our cause is at its ebb.
How could you go and do it!
    You've bothered Mr. Webb!
You came and asked for freedom,
    (As law does not forbid)
Not thinking it might bother him,
    And yet, it seems, it did.

Oh, can it be, my sisters,
    My sisters can it be,
You did not think of Mr. Webb
    When asking to be free?
You did not put his comfort
    Before your cause? How strange!
But now you know the way he feels
    I hope we'll have a change.

Send word to far Australia
    And let New Zealand know,
And Oregon and Sweden,
    Finland and Idaho;
Make all the nations grasp it,
    From Sitka to El Teb,
We never mention suffrage now;
    It bothers Mr. Webb!

The Spell

"The debutantes are entertained."

—Headline

The debutantes are entertained,
 Though Europe sink in smoke and blood
 And every hope of womanhood
Is there endangered, twisted, stained—
The debutantes are entertained.

The debutantes are entertained,
 Though many women young as they
 In this free country day by day
Are underfed and overstrained—
The debutantes are entertained.

O, lovely creatures, young and kind,
 How long, how long ere you rebel
 Against this tyranny, this spell
That dims the mirror of your mind
And keeps you debutantes—and blind!

THE SCALLOPS' CAMPAIGN SONG

"That great constructive piece of legislation, the Thompson bill, defining an 'adult' scallop, passed the Senate today without one dissenting vote."

—Evening Post, April 15, 1916

Oh, sister scallops, rejoice,
    Tyranny ends at last;
Without a dissenting voice,
    The scallop bill has passed!

Never again in the briny
    Waters near shore
Shall a scallop, timid and tiny,
    Tremble as heretofore—
Tremble and start and wake
To the sound of scoop and rake,
The terrible means men take
    Now nevermore, nevermore.

In a quiet, scalloplike manner
    We worked for our bill;
Never a ball or banner,
    Nor nagging, nor talk, until
The Senate, wholly at leisure,
Made it their pride and pleasure
To pass the scallops' measure—
    The better scallops' will.

Then perished party passion
    When it was understood
That scallops, in good old fashion,
    Were not too clever for food.
For the power of scallops is much;
And men will yield at a touch
Of scallops acting as such,
    True to their scallophood.

Is It Like This in Brooklyn?

*"Instinctively we think of woman as a creature to be coddled, and not
to be excited emotionally."*

—Editorial, Brooklyn Eagle

I think my cook a creature to be coddled,
    To my laundress I know just the things to say,
And my bearing to my scrubwoman is modelled
    On the bedside manner of a better day.
To the women in my factory I mention
    What divine and fragile flowers women are,
And my constant intervention spares my typist nervous tension,
    And my switchboard girl has never known a jar.

POOR THINGS

"They are for holding their notions though all men be against them, but I am for religion in what, and so far as, the times and my safety will bear it. They are for Religion when in rags and contempt; but I am for him when he walks in silver slippers in the sunshine and with applause."

—"Pilgrim's Progress"

Oh, alas, for all the women
    Who are converts to our cause,
But who wait for silver slippers,
    And for sunshine and applause.

Oh, alas, for all the people
    Who can feel and reason straight,
But who always get in action
    Just a little bit too late.

Just too late to make their gesture
    Something splendid and sincere,
Just too late because it's patent
    That the victory is here.

Oh, alas, for those who forfeit
    What can never come again—
The delight of having struggled,
    In contempt and in the rain.

The Safest Place

"No woman in the state has been insulted, beaten, choked or murdered at the polls. Since the vote has been bestowed on the women of Illinois all these things have happened to women in their own homes."

—Rheta Childe Dorr, in The New York Evening Mail

Go out to the polls, my Mary,
    For a girl is safer there
Than she is in any place on earth.
    But if you stay home, beware!
It's dangerous up on a ladder,
    Dangerous lighting a stove;
When Aunt was hanging the clothesline out
    Five stories down she dove.

It's a risky place, my Mary,
    Though both of us hold it dear;
But more women die at home, you know,
    Than anywhere else each year.
So don't stay home, my darling,
    Get used to your vote in youth;
For no one ever heard of a girl
    Who died in the polling booth.

On the Woman's Account

"The ———— National Bank values the woman's account. True, a woman ordinarily has not at her command and disposition funds in the amount customarily handled by a man, but the aggregate of a number of women's accounts is useful to a bank. . .

"The ———— National Bank maintains a separate department for women's accounts, with a maid in attendance, and a businesslike but courteous service."

—Adv.

*   *   *   *   *   *

It's a proud day, my sisters,
    For all the female clans;
A bank will take our money,
    As if it were a man's!
In a pioneering spirit
    They'll accept it,—cash or checks,
Our timid, trifling money,
    Money of the weaker sex.

Our gold seems just as golden,—
    Or so these flatterers say—
Our ounce of silver weighs as much
    As any man's could weigh;
And our long, long green ones,
    And our crisp, crisp yellows,
Are just about as valuable
    As any other fellow's.

Oh, happy days, my sisters,
    Oh, give these bankers thanks,
Who for our sake will even take
    Our money in their banks;

Nor are they cross about it;
    They neither scratch nor strike;
They take it in a manner,
    "Courteous, but businesslike."

*   *   *   *   *   *

The Indirect Influence

"The travelling men of New York are asking for legislation which will enable them to vote—that is to say, to enable them to register although absent from their residence."

Travelling men, what is the matter?
    Why this unrest and alarm?
Can't you cajole, coax or flatter?
    Can't you depend on your charm?
How can you say, even in play,
You need a ballot to get your own way!

Charm is what statesmen kotow to,
    Charm is their rise and their fall,
Votes they would never allow to
    Alter their conduct at all.
Charm is your dower; cling to that power.
Votes is a pleasure that fades in an hour.

ALICE DUER MILLER

"What Is Coming"

"There can be no question that the behaviour of the great mass of women in Great Britain has not simply exceeded expectation but hope. And there can be as little doubt that the suffrage question, in spite of the self-advertising violence of its extravagant section, did contribute very materially to build up the confidence, the willingness to undertake responsibility and face hardship that has been so abundantly displayed by every class of woman. . . At every sort of occupation they have been found efficient beyond precedent and intelligent beyond precedent. There is scarcely a point where women, having been given a chance, have not more than made good. . . These women have won the vote."

—From "What Is Coming," by H. G. Wells

Oh, Mr. Wells, your words sound very nice,
Yet if efficiency and sacrifice
Could win the vote for women, don't you know
We should have won it many years ago?

In every battle that was ever fought
In war or industry or law or thought,
Men have received with wondering delight
The help their women gave them in the fight:
But after war there is no other debt
That men it seems so easily forget.
Therefore I fear the Englishman will say
In the old scornful, ante-bellum way:
"Women are kind and good, hardworking, too,
But women, voting—that would hardly do!
Besides they do not want the vote, one hears."
And when they cry "We do!" he'll stop his ears.

OUR FRIENDS

Inez Milholland Boissevain

We do not talk of martyrs, no, not we
Who daily watch the long and bloody toll
Taken by war and industry, and see
How common is this gallantry of soul;
We do not talk of martyrs, we who plead
To share the duties of a human lot,
Who hold the faith that Truth and Honour lead
Along a path where women falter not;
We do not talk of martyrs; yet when one
So young, so eager, and so brave departs,
Her cause unconquered, and her task undone,
A sacred bitterness is in our hearts!
    How long must we be patient under wrong?
    Alas, my countrymen, how long, how long!

To the New Converts

Ladies, whose conversions date
  Rather late,
Who but now have understood
That the cause of womanhood
Is not alien, and unknown,
  But your own.

Ladies, who can recollect,
  I suspect,
That you once stood by and mocked,
And were elegant and shocked,
And were haughty and remote
  From the vote.

Just because in bygone years
  Your own sneers,
Your own clinging with such passion
To the side you thought the fashion
Made the work so hard to do
  For the few.

Now, when everything is pleasant,
  As at present,
Now that ridicule is not
Universally our lot,
Now that every public man
Tries to please us all he can,
Ladies, don't you think you owe
More, because you were so slow?
Just because you used to shirk,
  Get to work!

Fable of the Bird and the Sages

Some Eastern prophets, elderly and sage,
Were walking in a wood one summer day,
When suddenly they came upon a cage
Holding a long-winged bird of plumage gay;
    And, as this seemed to them a curious thing,
    They sat down to discuss it in a ring.

They made their discourse under headings three:
First, was the cage its natural habitat?
Next, could it fly, if they should set it free?
Last, would it change, then, to a mole or cat?
    Each had a theory, evolved or heard,
    On the essential nature of a bird.

The argument continued many years,
Until one day a youth came strolling by,
To whom they told their questions and their fears.
"Easy to answer them," he made reply.
    "Easy!" cried they. "How can you take it thus?
    How can you answer what is hid from us?"

"Like this," said he, "and all your wisdom's store
Would never find so clear an answer, friends."
And, stepping to the cage's gilded door,
He opened it. And there the story ends.
    The moral is: To know if birds will fly,
    The surest method is to let them try.

To 1915

Good-bye, Old Year, you were a teacher stern
In aim, and in your method most severe,
Yet every lesson you have made us learn
Will shape the story of the coming year;
How those first precepts of our country's youth,
Though we have heard they were an empty phrase,
Are still to many men a living truth
By which democracy must guide her ways;
You taught us, not our friends and foes alone,
But how friends hinder, and how foes may aid;
You taught us what ourselves had never known—
Our strength; you taught us not to be afraid;
  But most you taught that freedom has a price,
  And comes, but comes not without sacrifice.

　　　　　　　　　　　　　ALICE DUER MILLER

New Year's Resolutions for Suffragists

L et us resolve to remember:

1. That we are working for suffrage because of our own convictions on the subject, and not as a personal favour to the chairman of some committee.
2. That no one else is ideally fitted to do the job assigned to us, so we might as well attend to it ourselves.
3. That no one else will suffer any less in doing it than we do; they may talk less about their suffering.
4. That, as some day we shall undoubtedly say: "Yes, I was one of the women who worked hard for suffrage," we might as well work hard.
5. That it is unnecessary to be either apologetic or antagonistic about the cause, but if we must be one or the other, the latter is preferable.
6. That the only way to get rest from suffrage work is to get suffrage.

Reflections of a Suffragist

And Perhaps of an Anti

If my heart sinks at thought of a campaign
      Again,
It is not that I'm lazy, that I shirk
      Hard work,
It is not that it makes me faint and weak
      To speak,
Nor that I find it such a horrid plague
      To beg,
Not that I fear the strain of being quite
      Suavely polite
To many whom I'd so much rather smite,
      Or bite;
It isn't even that I hate and fear
      To hear
The "facts" of our opponents year by year;
      But, dear, oh, dear,
It is the weary things that day by day
      I'll have to say;
The things the voters ought to know, and don't,
      Or won't,
About democracy, the home, the wife,
      The mother's life,
Responsibility, the schools, pure food,
      And womanhood.
That's the necessity that I deplore—
      Saying once more
The things that every one has said before.
      My, what a bore!

Rules for Delegates

When ladies in convention meet
They must be civil, suave and sweet,
Must all be lovely to each other
And never say a word like "bother,"
For if one woman should be heard
To use that short, improper word,
It would be proof, you must admit,
That every woman was unfit.

When ladies in convention meet
Their harmony must be complete;
United they must think the same
Of every method, date and aim,
For if they do not all agree
They are not ready to be free.
You never knew a man's convention
Distracted by the least dissension.

When ladies in convention meet
They must be handsome, young and neat;
That is, if they would not forget
The precedents that men have set;
For men's conventions do their duty
By calmness, harmony and beauty.
Just wait until next June and you
Can see if what I say is true.

April, 1916

A Mother to Her Son

On His Request for a Latchkey

Why should you want a key, dearie,
    What do you want it for?
Mother is always ready and glad
    To get up and open the door.
If you'd a latchkey, Georgie,
    Mightn't it just destroy
The charm of the whole relation
    Between a mother and boy?

A woman likes her offspring
    To cling, and who can tell—
If you could open the door yourself
    I might not love you as well.
Waiting upon you, Georgie,
    Is such a pleasure to me,
I shouldn't enjoy life half so much
    If you were given a key.

You think that's rather selfish?
    Georgie, my dear, please note,
It's word for word what you said to me
    Of giving women the vote.
The ballot you think is different
    To giving a boy a key?
Well, think it over again, my son,
    And see if we can't agree.

ALICE DUER MILLER

HER SPHERE

When wives were quite unprecedented
    In Eden, where that fruit tree grew;
When Eve, that is, was just invented
    And even Man was rather new,
A good idea occurred to Adam,
    A theory and a practice, too;
"Your sphere," he said, "will be, dear Madam,
    To bear the blame for what I do."

A Possible Solution

Ladies, who of course admire
      (And inspire
      Now and then,)
Flowery phrases, words of fire,
   On the lips of public men,
Never feel the least compunction
      For an unction
      Insincere;
Admiration is your function,
   Blandishment your highest sphere.
Praise us always to our faces,
      But in cases,
      I implore,
Praise us less in public places,
   And at home a little more.

JOHN T. MAY

Into the office of John T. May
A suffragist came on his busy day.

"I've come to ask of you, sir," said she,
"What may your views on suffrage be?"

The great man scowled, as a great man should,
Facing rebellious womanhood.
"This interview," he said, "is closed.
I am unalterably opposed."

"At least," said she, "you'll consent to say
Why you oppose us, Mr. May."

The great man raised his hand in the air:
"While sun and moon are shining there,
While man looks up to the azure dome,
So long will the woman's place be home."

The suffragist did not blanch or blink,
She did not tremble or start or shrink.
She said: "Well, well, it must be confessed
Your thought is admirably expressed,
Forceful, coherent, and clear as day,
But will you stand by it, Mr. May?"

Never has printed page conveyed
The wonderful speech the great man made.
He spoke of policemen and charm and strength,
Of Nature's purpose he spoke at length,
He mentioned the Pilgrims' high intent,
Referred again to the firmament,
To angels and mothers, and queens and wives,
To the Bible, the flag and soldiers' lives,
To pedestals, roses and Bunker Hill,
And something he said of Jack and Jill.

Never a book of rhetoric teaches
So grand a speech among all the speeches.

Grave was the look on the stranger's face,
And she eyed her host for a minute's space.
Then she answered: "I see you are quite sincere
In the views you hold of woman's sphere;
Therefore I'll tell you before I go
Something the world will shortly know:
This is our secret, this is our news:
Most of us women share your views!"
The great man smiled, in a great wise way.
"I always knew it," said John T. May.

"Yes, home is our place," said she, "we know,
Now we intend to make it so.
Back to the home for womanhood;
That is our motto."
         And May said: "Good!"

Then the suffragist went on to tell
How their league was organised very well.
"Every girl in your factory, sir,
Feels that home is the place for her;
There she will go on a certain day,
Not a wheel will turn—"
         "Hold on," said May,
"That seems to me a different case."

"But why, if home is the woman's place?
Your filing clerks, and your typist, too,
Your telephone girls all think like you.
The women teachers, thousands strong,
Think they have left the home too long.
The libraries will all be closed and then
The stage will be peopled by men—just men.
All the women who sell in shops,
All the women who clean with mops,

Cooks and housemaids will all obey
The wonderful words of John T. May."

Silent awhile the great man stood,
And really thought, as a great man should;
Thought for the first time clearly and rightly
About that phrase he had used so lightly;
Saw, though he hadn't before conceived it.
As a matter of fact he'd never believed it,
Never had thought of their homes, 'twas true,
If he had work for women to do.

And his smile was sudden and shrewd and gay:
"I get you, madam," said John T. May.

INDEPENDENCE DAY

A Patriotic Hymn for Girls

Come, little girls, and let me teach
    The truths of Independence Day,
Lest patriotic song and speech
    Should lead your little minds astray,
Lest you should fancy you would be
Extolled for wishing to be free.

You've learnt whence governments derive
Their powers—their just powers, rather;
And how your fathers had to strive
    (But never imitate your father),
And how we've all enjoyed since then
Democracy—at least for men.

Learn now that each familiar phrase
    Does not refer to such as you,
And when you sing your country's lays
    Amend them thus, to make them true:
"Let freedom reign"—o'er all our brothers;
"Sweet land of liberty"—for others.

OUR FRIEND THE ENEMY

Love Sonnets of an Anti-Suffragist

I

TO HIS LOVE, COMPLIMENTING HER ON HER LACK OF INTELLIGENCE

Mabel, my love burns with this flame intense,
Not for your beauty, though I find you fair,
Not for your charming lack of common sense,
Not for your ignorance, beyond compare.
I love you, not because I think your mind
Is empty as a flawless cup of glass,
Not for the fascination that I find
Hearing you talking like a perfect ass.
No, but because with you, as in a dream,
I seem a giant, dominant and strong,
As in real life I very seldom seem,
Or only after effort hard and long,
    But you admire everything I do,
    And all I say you greet with, "Oh, how true!"

II

TO HIS LOVE, COMPLIMENTING HER ON HER LACK OF CIVIC RESPONSIBILITY

I praise you, Mabel, that your woman's heart
Is all untouched by tales of woe and crime,
And that you have no wish to bear your part
In curing any evil of the time.
I bless you that you are so unaware
Of infant children labouring in our mills,
And that you really do not seem to care
For other women's injuries and ills.
I love you when they tell you ugly things
Of death and poverty about your door,
You fold your hands with all their flashing rings,

Fixing on me the eyes that I adore,
    And say in accents like a silver bell:
    "What matter, Ferdinand, if you are well!"

III

TO HIS LOVE, SUGGESTING A CONGENIAL TOPIC

Come, Mabel, let us spend a pleasant hour
Telling what silly creatures women are.
Will not that be delectable, my Flower,
My Angel-Princess, Queen and Guiding Star?
Come, let us two Olympians be gay,
Jesting about your sex's lack of truth,
Their cowardice, their vanity, the way
They cling, though agéd, to the garb of youth;
Their mental powers, charming, but absurd;
Their inability to do or plan;
And then, my darling, you may say your word
In praise of that supreme creation, Man.
    What's that you say? That not all men are great?
    Your thought, my Mabel, savours of sex-hate.

IV

TO HIS LOVE, REPROACHING HER WITH AN UNKINDNESS

O, Mabel, you have wounded me beyond
All words—have dimmed our love's initial splendour;
I, who had thought you faithful, reverent, fond,
Am filled with doubts of your complete surrender.
Last evening when the argent car of night
Went up the sky with many a starry minion,
You, without asking me if you were right,
Expressed a clear, impersonal opinion,
A judgment, a belief, an abstract thought;
And though I frowned and held myself aloof,
And murmured sternly: "Nothing of the sort,"

You did not seem to notice the reproof.
    O, Mabel, cease to think, or how can we
    Be certain we shall never disagree?

V

TO HIS LOVE, SUGGESTING A MORE DISCRIMINATING TIMIDITY

How sweet and womanly to me you seemed
When first we met in that old silent house,
And suddenly you clung to me and screamed,
Your tender heart affrighted by a mouse.
But when today, afar, I saw you pass,
Walking with one I never fancied much,
And when you found a serpent in the grass,
And caught his hand with that same frantic clutch,
And did not shrink from his protecting arm,
Which instantly about your shoulder stole,
I, in my heart, exclaimed: "This is not charm!
This is the merest lack of self-control!"
    O, Mabel, learn to mitigate your fear—
    At least when any other man is near!

VI

TO HIS LOVE, EXPLAINING THE INDIRECT INFLUENCE

A woman's highest power is to please,
Thus does she rule the kingdom of the soul.
Beauty, charm, grace—when Heaven gave her these
It gave her Life's full, absolute control.
All forms of force are impotent and crude
Compared to this, which bends us to her whim.
Mabel, there is no man so vile and rude
But woman's tender grace may tutor him.
But now, my darling, use not any more
This power of yours on any other men—
Not on that sleek and handsome Senator

To whom you talked from eight till half-past ten.
    Use it on me, my love, and you will find
      How hard it is to change a strong man's mind.

Impressions at a Recent Anti Meeting

One Male Speaker.   A Chorus of Lady-Antis.

SPEAKER: I am cleverer than you.
CHORUS: Very true, very true.
SPEAKER: I am braver, too, by far.
CHORUS: So you are, so you are.
SPEAKER: I can use my mind a lot.
CHORUS: We cannot, we cannot.
SPEAKER: Men adore your lack of mind.
CHORUS: Oh, how kind; oh, how kind!
SPEAKER: You do very well without.
CHORUS: Not a doubt, not a doubt.
SPEAKER: You have hardly any sense.
CHORUS: What eloquence, what eloquence!
SPEAKER: Yet your moral sense is weaker.
CHORUS: Isn't he a charming speaker!

The Anti Speaks

In the subway I have never stood a minute,
    I have never clung an instant to a strap;
As I enter any train, each man who's in it
    Springs, like Galahad awaking from a nap,
And exclaims with hat in hand:
"I can't bear to see you stand;
    If you voted, though, I shouldn't care a rap."

O you women who have never stood in trolleys
    (And I speak to every woman in this state)
If you don't forego these wild and wicked follies,
    You'll be very, very sorry, but too late;
Men, disgusted at your capers,
Will sit still and read their papers,
    And you'll have to stand in trolleys. What a fate!

For myself, my only means of locomotion
    Is my motor, which conveys me near and far,
But I talk with men I know, and get a notion,
    From their logical account, just how things are;
And they say if women voted
Dreadful changes would be noted—
    Men might even let us stand up in a car!

The Happy Obstructionist

"Oh, no, I don't approve of giving women the vote.
        Women," he said, "are something divine, apart,
Something mysterious, precious, fair and remote,
        Caring for nothing but love, religion and art."

                "But women are really not like that," said I.
                "I like to think of them so," was his reply.

"I like to think of the mother, serene, at ease,
        Living her life in a sunny, vine-clad cot,
Drawing her happy babies about her knees,
        Teaching them love—for that is a mother's lot."

                "But very few mothers can live like that," said I.
                "But I like to picture them thus," was his reply.

"Think of the women," I said, "who suffer and toil,
        Of her without beauty or love, not mother or wife."
"Hush, hush," he answered, "why do you want to spoil
        The vision, the joy, the whole romance of life!"

                "But truth has its own romance and joy," said I.
                "I like my fancies better," was his reply.

Marriage

According to the New York Board of Education

DEDICATED TO MRS. ELIZABETH ELDREDGE

Oh, the tragedy, the pity!
  Oh, the things that women do!
There's a rumour in the city,
  But we hope it isn't true;
There's a scandal has been carried,
  And the clubs are whispering
That a teacher has been married—
  Isn't that a shocking thing?

Marriage in our estimation
  For a man is not a crime,
And the Board of Education
  Will not dock his pay or time;
But a woman is a lily;
  Marriage is not in her line;
For an act so weak and silly
  We must ask her to resign.

A Politician to the Ladies

Please go away. I am so very tired;
    My working day is long;
I try to do the job for which I'm hired.
    Alas! I am not strong.

I've seen so many men today, requesting
    So many things to do:
And now you come, just as I might be resting,
    And want to see me, too.

Ladies, I don't approve of suffrage, really
    (Though it may come at length);
Women must base their hopes of progress merely
    On Man's heroic strength!

Antis We Have Known

I

An anti, fair and apparently tender,
Sat with her feet on her own brass fender;
Safe as a human life can be
From want and suffering, so safe was she,
Safe by money and social position,
By love and learning and sound tradition;
Never a stroke of work had she done,
Never a dollar earned or won,
Her children in school, and her husband gone
To his office, she sat by her fire alone
With time to read the election news,
And found it exactly met her views.
She was glad the women had been defeated,
That was the way they ought to be treated;
Glad that women who toiled all day
Were not to be equals in any way;
Glad that women she passed in the street
Couldn't in any way compete;
Glad, since wisdom and wealth and power
Guarded her children every hour,
To know that tenement mothers and wives
Couldn't help guard their children's lives;
Glad since everything suited her
That other women should stay as they were.
Which shows that being secure, apart,
Petted and sheltered by every art,
Doesn't develop the human heart.

November 4, 1915

II

"My principal reason against it," said he,
"Is that women don't want it, as far as I see."

"O Father," his daughter exclaimed, "is that true?
You know that I want it, and Mother does, too."

He smiled with omniscience peculiar to him:
"My darling," he said, "that is only a whim."

"But it isn't a whim," she replied, "in Miss Hays,
Who writes all your letters. You frequently praise
Her poise and good sense; well, she wants it, she says."

"Do you think that her judgment or mine is the ripest?"
He asked. "Must I learn how to vote from my typist?"

"Well, then," she went on, "all the teachers at school
Are for it."

He laughed. "I have found as a rule
That all of the unmarried women I've known
Want nothing so much as a home of their own;
If all of your teachers were married, you'd note
A striking decrease in their wish for the vote."

"Many teachers are married," she started to say,
But he begged she would not contradict in that way.

"You're growing," he said, "both aggressive and vain.
I think we won't mention this subject again."

That night at the club they were speaking of It,
And he said that he wasn't opposed—not a bit.

"It is true I am voting against it," said he;
"But the women I know do not want it, you see."

Verbatim

"I love my home," the Anti said,
"I crave no interests in its stead.
You think that foolish, I dare say—
Yes—I'm peculiar, in a way,
And so I must admit I do
Adore my home and children, too.
And, oh, I love my husband, though
You suffragists will sneer, I know.
I am not clever, and I fear
I do not make my meaning clear,
But what I'm trying to express
Is this: I love my home. Confess,
You think it very crude and silly
To love my little tots and Billy,
But yet I do—I think I ought—
I wonder if you catch my thought?"

ALICE DUER MILLER

Her Representative

"I represent my wife," he said;
    "I really cannot see
How she would profit by the vote;
    I vote for her and me.
And men consider—Time has shown—
Their wives' opinions like their own.

"If my wife voted she would vote
    For many silly measures,
Which do not add in any way
    To profits or to pleasures;
Like Widows' Pensions, Equal Pay,
More schools, and an eight-hour day.

"On Woman Suffrage I vote no;
    Perhaps you had not heard
My wife believes in that as well;
    How wicked and absurd!
Oh, let us save domestic strife,
And let me represent my wife!"

A Son to His Anti-Suffrage Mother

Mother, dear mother, how could you deceive me!
    Where shall I find consolation and balm?
"Willie," you always have taught me, "believe me,
    Women who vote never have any charm."

Out of the West came a beautiful stranger;
    Fast beat my heart, but I felt no alarm;
Why should I fear an impossible danger?
    Stella had voted—she couldn't have charm.

Much of my time at her side I expended,
    Trying to teach her a woman's true place.
Sometimes she yawned, twice or thrice was offended.
    Once, I assure you, she laughed in my face.

Stella has plighted her word to another;
    Told me the news with the cruellest calm,
Added: "There, Willie, run home to your mother;
    Tell her that Cave Men are losing their charm."

Ode

Recollection of Anti-Suffrage Speeches Heard in Early Childhood

With apologies to W. W.

Admit at the beginning
That woman is no good.
You find that very winning?
Ah, yes; I thought you would.

I

There was a time when platform, stage and hall,
Speeches, at least in public view,
      Did me appal;
   They were to me taboo,
Not woman's sphere at all.
It is not now as once it was; I roam
      Where'er I may
      By night or day,
To preach to Man that Woman's place is home.

II

     The fashion comes and goes,
     As everybody knows;
     Feathers on a last year's hat
   Are raggedy to wear;
     The white, or lemon, spat
     Is beautiful and fair;
   Large plaids are not refined;
   It's clear to me—and you agree—
That these are tasks enough for woman's mind.

III

The vote is but a fraud and a deception;
    The way to get our will, the way to win
Is not at an election,
       But darkly, with a grin.
Not quite without protection,
Not in complete subjection,
But armed with charms superlative we come
      To each secluded home.
Thanks to the votes we are too good to cast,
Thanks to the news we have not read for years,
We all assume that every law that's passed
Is due to our unshed, but potent, tears.

ALICE DUER MILLER

To the Anti-Campaigners

Antis, for Wilson so gladly campaigning,
    Antis campaigning so gaily for Hughes,
Would you object very much to explaining
    What in the world are your views?

You whose conviction could never be shaken:
    Voting incited a woman to roam;
Do I not see you—or am I mistaken—
    Voteless, but far from the home?

Woman's inferior, so you insisted;
    Over her faults and her failings you gloat.
Haven't you got things a little bit twisted,
    Teaching these men how to vote?

You, who have told them their wives and their mothers
    Had not political wisdom, you knew;
Why should they think you more wise than the others?
    Why should they listen to *you?*

UNAUTHORISED INTERVIEWS

An Unauthorised Interview

Between the Suffragists and the Statue of Liberty

The Suffragists

Lady robed in light,
    At our harbour standing,
Equal law and right
    Promising, demanding,
Can you tell us, do you know,
Why you treat your daughters so?

Do not think us pert,
    Insolent or teasing,
But you seem a flirt,
    Only bent on pleasing
That one-half of human kind
Who made Sister Justice blind.

The Statue

Be not deceived, my daughters, I'm not she—
The wingèd Goddess, who sets nations free.
I am that Liberty, which when men win
They think that others' seeking is a sin;
I am that Liberty which men attain
And clip her wings lest she should fly again:
I am that Liberty which all your brothers
Think good for them and very bad for others.
Therefore they made me out of bronze, and hollow,
Immovable, for fear that I might follow
Some fresh rebellion, some new victim's plea;
And so they set me on a rock at sea,
Welded my torch securely in my hand
Lest I should pass it on, without command.
I am a milestone, not an inspiration;
And if my spirit lingers in this nation,

If it still flickers faintly o'er these waters,
It is your spirit, my rebellious daughters.

Queens and Goddesses

SCENE: *Congress, during a woman suffrage debate. The Congressmen are, as usual, moving about, talking, reading, dozing, and one, an anti-suffragist, is speaking.*

CONGRESSMAN: I shall vote "No" on this measure, but I wish to
  say I take
  My stand for Woman's protection, for her own sake.
  No one honours Woman, no one respects her more,
  Than I do; as queen and goddess I love and adore—
(Suddenly in an open space in front of the Speaker's desk appear Pallas Athene and Cleopatra)
CLEOPATRA: Strange little man without weapons, what can you mean?
PALLAS: I, in my time, was a goddess—
CLEOPATRA: And I was a queen.
PALLAS: Men knelt with gifts at my altar, gifts of ivory and gold,
  Bowls of bronze and of silver chased by the tools of old.
  No council of chiefs was held, no treaty or war begun
  But they prayed to me for wisdom—
CLEOPATRA: And all that I wished was done.
PALLAS: My name was spoken with reverence, for the mortal's breath
  That jests on the name of a goddess calls soon for death.
  But here one spoke of his goddess, likening her to a hen.
  Think you Immortals suffer such words from the lips of men?
CLEOPATRA: And one was talking of queens for many an hour,
  Till I longed to clap my hands with their old, old power
  And cry "Come hither, my guards, take this old man away,
  For his ignorant talk of queens wearies your queen today."
PALLAS (*more kindly*): If you have each a goddess, as all of you boast,
  Hurry and bring her here, here, where you need her most.
  She must be strong and wise; while ye, O mortals, are weak.
  Pray that she come and save you, from the foolish words
    you speak.
  If you have each a goddess—
CONGRESSMAN (*recovering from his astonishment*): Yes, but home is her
  shrine.
PALLAS: Ah, I have seen those shrines, lovely, many, as mine,

But women are toiling in them, toiling like slaves.

Are they your goddesses?

CONGRESSMAN (*confused*): Yes.

CLEOPATRA: Surely the old man raves!

I know the fate of captives and slaves of the East:

They must work till they die, or are sold like a beast.

This man owns them by thousands. They toil amid wheels that grind.

They are his slaves.

CONGRESSMAN (*faintly*): No, queens.

CLEOPATRA (*angrily*): The man is mad or blind.

PALLAS: Nay, nay, Daughter of Egypt, he is neither blind nor mad,

But talking as men still talk when their cause is bad.

To cover an ugly truth he uses a pretty phrase

As even the Gods have done in the good old days.

He knows that the woman who toils for some one else to be rich

Is no more a queen than the man who digs a ditch.

He knows that the wife at home, whom he does, as he says, revere,

Is not a goddess, or else he would seek her counsel here.

He knows her merely a woman, and he wants no woman to share

His power—

CLEOPATRA: Why does he not say so?

PALLAS: Because he does not dare.

CLEOPATRA: Dares not? Is he a coward?

PALLAS: Nay, he fears where he ought.

For as some men think of women they are wise to hide their thought.

(She turns to Congressman)

Mortal, I am a goddess. Do not tremble and shrink.

I read your heart about women—all that you wish and think.

Base it is, and unworthy, but I strike you not dead at my feet.

This is my sentence upon you—a punishment meet—

When you tell your thought of Woman, you shall tell the truth.

How you despise her wholly—all but her beauty and youth.

Henceforth when you speak of Woman, you shall tell all your heart.

CONGRESSMAN (*terrified*): I must be silent forever! *(A pause)*

PALLAS TO CLEOPATRA: Come, Queen, we may now depart.

ALICE DUER MILLER

IMPRESSIONS OF A CANVASSER

SCENE: *A Certain State Capitol.*

CHARACTERS

SUFFRAGISTS. *Half a dozen Legislators Opposed.*

SUFFRAGISTS: Please, sir, to tell us, if you will,
How you will vote upon our bill?
1ST LEGISLATOR: Ladies, observe my easy grace,
My manners and my pleasant face;
I hope you see I bow, I smile,
I call you "ladies"—all the while
My heart is black with seething hate
That I, who am so very great,
Should have to waste a single minute
On your affairs—there's nothing in it.
SUFFRAGISTS (*to another legislator*): And you, sir, if we recollect,
Are much opposed. Is that correct?
2ND LEGISLATOR: Opposed! O ladies, no, indeed!
I vote against you, I concede;
I may continue so to do,
But I am not *opposed* to you.
To call me so is most unjust.
I make myself quite plain, I trust.
SUFFRAGISTS (*to another legislator*): And may we hear from you,
sir, how
You'll vote?
3RD LEGISLATOR: I have no option now;
I listen to my district's voice;
It voted no; I have no choice.
SUFFRAGISTS: O sir, I think there's some mistake,
Your district carried.
4TH LEGISLATOR (*hastily interrupting*): Let me make
His statement clear; he means that we
All come here absolutely free.
Not at our districts' beck and nod,

We vote to please ourselves and God;
And we are not in all events
The slaves of our constituents.

SUFFRAGISTS (*slightly puzzled, to another legislator*): And you, sir, shall
 you vote for it?

5TH LEGISLATOR: No, though I think you will admit
 I have a very open mind;
 If in my district I should find
 The women want it (*which they don't*),
 I'd vote for it. Till then I won't.

SUFFRAGISTS: And have you asked so very many?

5TH LEGISLATOR (*astonished*): Why, no, I don't think I've asked any.

SUFFRAGISTS (*to another legislator*): And what, sir, is your attitude?

6TH LEGISLATOR: I hope you will not think me rude,
 If, ladies, as a friend I say
 You do not work the proper way.
 It's time you disappeared, and let
 The public utterly forget
 That there are women wish to vote.
 Then at some future time, remote,
 In twenty years, or twenty-five,
 If you should chance to be alive,
 You'd see a change—at least you ought—
 A striking change in public thought.
 This from a friend.

SUFFRAGISTS: But are you so?

6TH LEGISLATOR: A friend? Oh, well, I voted "no,"
 But surely you can comprehend
 That I advise you as a friend.

(*Suffragists alone*)

1ST SUFFRAGIST: The men in favour talk much less.

2ND SUFFRAGIST: They haven't much to say but "yes";
 The men opposed explain a lot
 How they're opposed and yet they're not.
 It takes some time to make that clear.

1ST SUFFRAGIST: How very bad the air is here!

2ND SUFFRAGIST: Do you refer to ventilation,
 Or to the general situation?

(*The reply is inaudible*)

         ALICE DUER MILLER

A Note About the Author

Alice Duer Miller (1874–1942) was an American novelist, poet, screenwriter, and women's rights activist. Born into wealth in New York City, she was raised in a family of politicians, businessmen, and academics. At Barnard College, she studied Astronomy and Mathematics while writing novels, essays, and poems. She married Henry Wise Miller in 1899, moving with him in their young son to Costa Rica where they struggled and failed to open a rubber plantation. Back in New York, Miller earned a reputation as a gifted poet whose satirical poems advocating for women's suffrage were collected in *Are Women People?* (1915). Over the next two decades, Miller published several collections of stories and poems, some of which would serve as source material for motion picture adaptations. *The White Cliffs* (1940), her final published work, is a verse novel that uses the story of a young women widowed during the Great War to pose important questions about the morality of conflict and patriotism in the leadup to the United States' entrance into World War II.

A Note from the Publisher

Spanning many genres, from non-fiction essays to literature classics to children's books and lyric poetry, Mint Edition books showcase the master works of our time in a modern new package. The text is freshly typeset, is clean and easy to read, and features a new note about the author in each volume. Many books also include exclusive new introductory material. Every book boasts a striking new cover, which makes it as appropriate for collecting as it is for gift giving. Mint Edition books are only printed when a reader orders them, so natural resources are not wasted. We're proud that our books are never manufactured in excess and exist only in the exact quantity they need to be read and enjoyed.

bookfinity™

Discover more of your favorite classics with Bookfinity™.

- Track your reading with custom book lists.
- Get great book recommendations for your personalized Reader Type.
- Add reviews for your favorite books.
- AND MUCH MORE!

Visit **bookfinity.com** and take the fun Reader Type quiz to get started.

Enjoy our classic and modern companion pairings!

Classic & Modern

Bookfinity is a registered trademark of Ingram Book Group LLC. © 2023 Bookfinity. All rights reserved.

www.ingramcontent.com/pod-product-compliance
Lightning Source LLC
Chambersburg PA
CBHW020602030426
42337CB00013B/1177